# There Came a Gy[illegible]

Frank McGuinness was born in Buncrana, Co. Donegal, and now lives in Dublin and lectures in English at University College Dublin. His plays include: *The Factory Girls* (Abbey Theatre, Dublin, 1982), *Baglady* (Abbey, 1985), *Observe the Sons of Ulster Marching Towards the Somme* (Abbey, 1985; Hampstead Theatre, London, 1986), *Innocence* (Gate Theatre, Dublin, 1986), *Carthaginians* (Abbey, 1988; Hampstead, 1989), *Mary and Lizzie* (RSC, 1989), *The Bread Man* (Gate, 1991), *Someone Who'll Watch Over Me* (Hampstead, West End and Broadway, 1992), *The Bird Sanctuary* (Abbey, 1994), *Mutabilitie* (NT, 1997), *Dolly West's Kitchen* (Abbey, 1999; Old Vic, 2000), *Gates of Gold* (Gate, 2002) and *Speaking Like Magpies* (RSC, 2005). His translations include Ibsen's *Rosmersholm* (NT, 1987) and *Peer Gynt* (Gate, 1988; RSC and international tour, 1994; NT, 2000), Chekhov's *Three Sisters* (Gate and Royal Court, 1990), Lorca's *Yerma* (Abbey, 1987, and Arcola, 2006), Brecht's *The Threepenny Opera* (Gate, 1991), *Hedda Gabler* (Roundabout Theatre, Broadway, 1994), *Uncle Vanya* (Field Day production, 1995), *A Doll's House* (Playhouse Theatre, Broadway, 1997), *The Caucasian Chalk Circle* (NT, 1997 and 2007), Sophocles' *Electra* (Donmar, Broadway, 1998), Ostrovsky's *The Storm* (Almeida, 1998), *The Wild Duck* (Abbey, 2003), Euripides' *Hecuba* (Donmar, 2004) and *Phaedra*, after Racine (Donmar, 2006).

*also by Frank McGuinness*

GATES OF GOLD
DOLLY WEST'S KITCHEN
MARY AND LIZZIE
SOMEONE WHO'LL WATCH OVER ME
MUTABILITIE
OBSERVE THE SONS OF ULSTER MARCHING TOWARDS THE SOMME
SPEAKING LIKE MAGPIES

FRANK McGUINNESS PLAYS ONE
(*The Factory Girls,*
*Observe the Sons of Ulster Marching Towards the Somme,*
*Innocence, Carthaginians, Baglady*)

FRANK McGUINNESS PLAYS TWO
(*Mary and Lizzie, Someone Who'll Watch Over Me,*
*Dolly West's Kitchen, The Bird Sanctuary*)

*Translations*
A DOLL'S HOUSE (Henrik Ibsen)
PEER GYNT (Henrik Ibsen)
ELECTRA (Sophocles)
THE STORM (Alexander Ostrovsky)
HECUBA (Euripides)
PHAEDRA (after Racine)

*Screenplays*
Brian Friel's DANCING AT LUGHNASA

THE DAZZLING DARK: NEW IRISH PLAYS
(edited by Frank McGuinness)

FRANK McGUINNESS

# There Came a Gypsy Riding

ff
*faber and faber*

First published in 2007
by Faber and Faber Limited
3 Queen Square, London WC1N 3AU

Typeset by Country Setting, Kingsdown, Kent CT14 8ES
Printed in England by Bookmarque, Croydon, Surrey



A CIP record for this book
is available from the British Library

978-0-571-23303-8

2 4 6 8 10 9 7 5 3 1

For Angela and Roselean Cassidy

**There Came a Gypsy Riding** was first performed at the Almeida Theatre, London, on 11 January 2007. The cast, in order of appearance, was as follows:

**Bridget** Eileen Atkins
**Louise** Elaine Cassidy
**Simon** Aidan McArdle
**Margaret** Imelda Staunton
**Leo** Ian McElhinney

*Directed by* Michael Attenborough
*Designed by* Robert Jones
*Lighting* Paul Pyant
*Sound* Paul Arditti

# Characters

**Leo McKenna**
a husband

**Margaret**
his wife

**Louise**
their daughter

**Simon**
their son

**Bridget**
a distant cousin

*The McKennas have a younger son, Gene, who is dead. He would have been twenty-one the weekend they gather here in the play.*

*The play is set in the west of Ireland. The time is now.*

# THERE CAME A GYPSY RIDING

# Act One

*Morning.*

*The magnificent early light of the west of Ireland.*

*It shines brilliantly on the causeway.*

*Inside the house the light is more subdued, but it is still alive, more threatening, more revealing than electric light could ever be.*

*There are two loft beds with a ladder up to them at one side of the kitchen.*

*There is a bedroom and bathroom not seen onstage.*

*There is a summer seat on the causeway.*

*The light catches Simon turning in his sleep, in his loft bed, his arm reaching out as if to catch something.*

*He relaxes, curling into a foetal position, his sheet tossed aside.*

*Louise irons on the kitchen table.*

*She puts the finishing touches to a man's shirt.*

*From offstage Bridget's voice is heard singing.*

**Bridget**

There came a gypsy riding, riding, riding,
There came a gypsy riding e-i-o.
What are you riding here for, here for, here for,
What are you riding here for, e-i-o?

*Louise quietly joins in the song.*

**Louise** Riding here to marry, marry, marry –

*Louise stops singing.*

*Bridget resumes the song.*

**Bridget**
Riding here to marry, marry, marry –
Riding here to marry, e-i-o.

*Bridget appears on the causeway.*
*She pushes a child's empty buggy.*
*She is dressed as a woman of her age and her place would be dressed although she does wear worn, pale pink wellingtons.*
*She continues singing as she slowly pushes the buggy along the causeway.*

Who are you going to marry, marry, marry,
Who are you going to marry, e-i-o?
Marry all your children, children, children,
Marry all your children, e-i-o.

*Simon wakes up in his bed.*

Here's your sixpence, here's your ring,
Goodbye, children, goodbye.

*Bridget, Louise and Simon sing together.*

**Trio**
Here's your sixpence, here's your ring,
Goodbye, children, goodbye.

*Bridget is now visible to Louise through the open door.*
*Louise continues ironing.*
*Simon rises slowly.*
*He pulls a pair of jeans over his boxers.*
*As the scene progresses he wears a T-shirt and trainers.*

**Louise** Jesus, that's an old one, Bridget. I've not heard 'The Gypsy Riding' since we were kids.

**Bridget** What time is it?

**Louise** It's nearly three o'clock, Bridget.

**Bridget** Are they not here yet – Margaret and Leo?

**Louise** They'll be here soon. They left Dublin at the break of day.

**Bridget** Is Margaret driving?

**Louise** Yes, Ma's driving. She goes slow.

**Bridget** So they've not arrived, Louise?

**Louise** No, Bridget – they'll be here soon.

**Bridget** Are you ironing? Jesus, I hope you never do that on a Sunday. If you do and you die, the mark of a hot iron will be burnt on your back. Can you imagine the agony of that? It's why I never learned to do it – ironing. I'm like your mother in that way. Lazy about a house. Maybe she's just slow. That's why she drives the way she does.

**Louise** Ma's many things, Bridget, but she's not lazy.

**Bridget** But she hates ironing, though – do you know why? Your father told me. In her grandparents' house, years ago, somebody left one heating on a chair. Your mother – she would have been seven years old – she sat on it. Scalded her arse red. Took the flesh from her left buttock. The poor bitch was purple. They all laughed at the wee fucker. All she could do was cry when they'd roar at her, 'Hi Margaret, how's your bum?' Imagine sitting on a hot iron, imagine being that stupid.

*Bridget points to the buggy.*

What do you make of this contraption?

*Louise leaves the ironing and looks at the buggy.*

I found it abandoned down on the shore. Somebody must have thrown it away. People are rotten with money these days. Waste not, want not – forget that philosophy.

People spend money like water. But am I not the lucky woman that they do? Isn't this grand for me? Look – I can just lean on it. It makes my walking far easier. Look –

*She wheels the buggy along the causeway.*

Do you see the speed of me?

**Louise** Very handy, Bridget.

**Bridget** Amn't I the right Stirling Moss?

**Louise** I don't know who Stirling Moss is, Bridget.

**Bridget** Do you know, pet, neither do I. He must have been somebody sometime. Isn't it desperate to forget things? I'm going to tell you this, Louise. I have to remind myself to remember that I'm waiting for the car. When I don't see it, I have to come here and tell you that I'm watching out for Margaret and Leo. I have to make sure I know they haven't arrived. You've to tell me they're coming. Because I forget – I would forget my own head if it weren't attached to my shoulders.

**Louise** You're lucky it is, then.

**Bridget** No, dear, occasionally it's not. Isn't that strange? I can be merrily walking along these roads. Mile upon mile, to and fro from my house. I look in front of me – there's my head half a mile in the distance, chatting nineteen to the dozen. I get the shock of my life.

**Louise** Aye – you must.

**Bridget** The best of it is – I'm always smiling. The good time girl who lost her head. I tell you, I'm visibly shaken. Who could have predicted this would have been my end? A woman decapitated – I tell you, I'm the new Jayne Mansfield. And unlike that poor unfortunate I can explain this sorry state of affairs. Do you know why this happened?

**Louise** Tell me why.

**Bridget** The girl can't help it. This girl can't help it. Had you looked at me forty years ago, you would have seen the future of rock and roll. Nobody did so. They missed out. But I didn't. That is why I always have a big laugh on my face and it far ahead of the rest of my body. I can only describe this in one of two ways. Either it's a miracle or I'm completely mad. God's never blessed me particularly. So I rule out the miracles. That leaves madness. I'll have to plump for that, and it's very much against my will. I've no sympathy for ladies who go ga-ga. I find it very suspicious the way they're always throwing up their skirts and wearing no drawers. If I want to attract a man, I'll use more than my bare arse.

**Louise** That's a useful tip – I'll remember.

**Bridget** You could do worse. Yes, madness – it has to be. And I know when it dates from. The day and hour I found him.

*Silence.*

Stretched out cold – on the shore. The White Strand. An Trá Bán, as we say in Gaelic. The empty shore. But it wasn't empty, it wasn't white – it was red, he was there, your brother. I was never the same. Never will be. Never again.

*Simon speaks in the bedroom above.*

**Simon** Bridget, for the love of Christ, please, don't be there to greet them with this.

**Bridget** And his wrists – that's what were red –

**Louise** Bridget, I can't –

**Bridget** Jesus, the red on the white strand – my cousin had taken his own life –

**Louise** Bridget, I beg you, please –

**Bridget** What am I thinking of?

*Silence.*

You don't want to see it. Of course not. Your poor, poor brother. The youngest of you all.

*Silence.*

The mistake. That's what me and your mother used to joke. I called him the last of the name. Yes, the last of the litter. We would laugh at him in his carry-cot. They bought this place for half-nothing the year before he was born. I helped them buy it. Jesus, I found it for them. They were family. Is that – how long is that? It must be twenty years or more?

*Louise and Simon speak in duet.*

**Duet** Twenty-two.

**Bridget** Refresh my memory. You and Simon were barely walking. So he would be –

**Louise** Twenty-one. This weekend. Well remembered, cousin.

**Bridget** Don't honour me with that close connection. So he would have been –

**Louise** Twenty-one. This weekend. Gene –

**Bridget** I see. That's why you're here. Dear Jesus, and I am rabbiting on about finding the poor boy. Poor Eugene.

**Louise** Poor Gene – we called him –

**Bridget** Who gives a fuck what you called him? It does not matter now. The poor child – he's gone. I'll be on my way. I'll call down to see them when they're settled. Was the house warm enough?

**Louise** It was perfect as always, Bridget –

**Bridget** Could you not have called up to tell me –

**Louise** You always get it ready – you spoil us –

**Bridget** I thought you might have called to my house –

**Louise** This is not the easiest of times –

**Bridget** Thanks – that's all I wanted you to say.

**Louise** You know we thank you.

**Bridget** I do my best. What more can I do?

*She moves on, wheeling the buggy, patting it.*

This is a wonderful find for me. Isn't it great the way you can depend on the sea? Who knows what it will throw up next? I believe it invented the wheel. I begrudge it that. I wish I had. Ah well, if wishes were granted, beggars would be horses.

*She looks at Louise.*

Do you know, I'd love to be a horse? I would have been happy as a horse. Why am I talking like this? It's down to the weather. Give your mother my compliments of the Christmas season.

**Louise** This is not December, woman, we're in the middle of July.

**Bridget** Dear God, isn't it all go? Time – time – I can't keep up with it. No, I was never the same. Since I found him. It was the red wrists. Red as a robin, a June robin. But no, no – he was dead. Suicide. He'd be twenty-one this weekend. My God, you'll shed some tears. You shouldn't. He didn't for you. Don't mind me, I'm an old fool. Look after Mammy and Daddy. Bye-bye.

*She wheels off the buggy.*
*There is a piercing cry of seagulls.*
*Louise starts in fear.*
*Simon has climbed down the ladder to the kitchen.*

**Simon** Has she left the scene of the crime?

**Louise** She has, yes.

**Simon** Did she go on about it?

**Louise** She did. And could you blame her? The poor woman. The shock of it, finding him. Fuck him.

**Simon** You're not being very nice –

**Louise** About my poor brother –

**Simon** Your poor, dead brother.

**Louise** I'm sick of my poor, dead brother. Sick of having to watch my mouth. I'm already sick of this weekend. Not allowed to speak my mind. Not allowed one drink. Why punish us –

**Simon** Not just us. They're punishing themselves. Can you believe it? Ma and Da on the wagon for nearly two years?

**Louise** A glass of wine might poison us. It might bring on the waterworks –

**Simon** And they might not stop.

**Louise** Mine have stopped, Simon.

**Simon** Let's get through it, Loui – just that alone, keep the peace.

*Louise goes back to the ironing.*

Is it a deal?

*She does not answer.*

It's why I wanted to come down a few days earlier. Just you and me. If you want to give off, do it to me.

**Louise** I will not indulge –

**Simon** It is not indulgence –

**Louise** To wallow –

**Simon** It is not –

**Louise** This weekend is wallowing, no matter what we say. I indulge in it for their sake.

*She sings.*

Twenty-one today,
Twenty-one today,
Never been twenty-one before,
He'll get the key to the door.

*Silence.*

Well, he'll get no key. He is not twenty-one. He is dead in his grave. We may fool ourselves with some fantasy he can hear us. He cannot. But we'll play the game. I will get through it, because you ask me. I will do as you wish. Keep the peace.

**Simon** You have to, Louise. Still fragile – very fragile – both of them.

*She stops ironing.*

**Louise** They're getting there. They're getting over it. She's settled well back in college. Dominating the English Department. He's recovered enough to keep expanding the empire. Jesus, I pity any poor bastard who tried to cross him during his mourning. As if any who worked for him would try –

**Simon** The man's heart was broken –

**Louise** His heart, yes, no denying that. But I know my father. A tear in one eye and a laser at the other ready to blast you away. Ready to decimate anyone who'd step out of line.

**Simon** He's a fair man. You saw the way they comforted him –

**Louise** At the funeral? From the bar managers down to the girls who collect the glasses? They were there in multitudes. They must really be terrified of him.

**Simon** Of Da? Don't be –

**Louise** When he's wounded, he might be at his worst. Who knows where he'd bite next? That's what links our mammy and daddy. Their great strength – they are decidedly unpredictable. And they are tough as rock.

**Simon** The rock breaks, Louise.

*She embraces him.*

**Louise** How do you survive us all? How are you a brother to this hardhearted Hannah? What have I done to deserve you, you soft lump of shite?

**Simon** No funny business, sister.

*He disengages himself.*

**Louise** Wouldn't it be great if it was as simple as that? A wee bit of incest. That's why he did it.

**Simon** You and Gene –

**Louise** I was thinking more of you and him. Sister and brother – old hat. I was imagining a spot of queer sex. We can put it all down to an excess of brotherly love. Everything neat and tidy.

**Simon** Sister, you have the mind of a sewer.

**Louise** That is true. I do hope you are queer. I want no woman coming between us. And I would take such delight in seducing your boyfriend.

*Margaret has entered the causeway.*
*She looks about the place.*

**Simon** I think I may disappoint you there, lady. I like to hang out –

**Louise** With girls – I know.

*Margaret sits on one of the seats.*

**Margaret** Well, we've avoided Bridget.

**Louise** And you never tried out my clothes. Gene did. Well, once he did.

**Margaret** That's a good omen.

**Simon** He dressed up as a woman?

**Louise** Not quite. I dressed him up. He was seven.

**Simon** Why did you do it?

**Louise** It was raining. Do you think it affected him? I doubt it. At least he spared us that sight. He wasn't stretched out in Mummy's chiffon.

**Simon** Can you see our mother in chiffon?

**Louise** Ma is more the tar-and-feather type. She goes for the primitive look. I remember once getting into a fight at school. I was battered. She saw my black eye and thought it was mascara. She said it suited me.

**Simon** What's keeping them?

**Louise** They'll be on time.

**Simon** You're right not to cook anything.

**Louise** You must remember – I can't boil an egg.

*Margaret rises from the seat.*
*They start to imitate her voice.*

**Simon** A perfectly boiled egg.

**Louise** Four and a half minutes.

**Simon** Not five minutes.

**Louise** Not four.

**Simon** Four and a half minutes.

**Louise** For a perfect boiled egg.

**Simon** Perfect.

**Margaret** Children, I hear you all.

**Louise** Hi ya, Ma, welcome.

**Simon** You drove here safe?

**Margaret** Are you three pups mocking your mother?

*Silence.*
*Louise puts a finger to Simon's lips.*

**Louise** Just me and Simon, Ma, acting the eejit, the two of us.

*Margaret registers shock at her forgetfulness.*

**Simon** Are you all right, Ma?

**Margaret** Of course I am. Yes, Simon – it's you.

**Louise** And me, Louise.

**Margaret** Of course it's Louise. Who else would it be?

**Louise** Who indeed?

*Simon gives her a warning look.*
*Louise pulls a face back at him.*
*Margaret enters the cottage.*

**Margaret** I am roasted. That car was like an oven. There was not a breath of air from here to Dublin. The heat of the day. Your father offered to drive for me. I ate the face off him. We didn't speak since we hit Mayo. I was dying to open a window, but he made no move to open his, so I wouldn't give him the satisfaction of air blowing through mine. Let him stew.

*She turns to Louise.*

I know you can hardly boil an egg, but do you think you could rise to a cup of tea?

**Louise** I might. Would you like some Earl Grey?

**Margaret** Would you like some vomit?

**Louise** What's wrong with Earl Grey?

**Margaret** Its distinctively smoky aroma. Jesus, it's like drinking an ashtray. If I liked Earl Grey, I would hardly have quit the cigarettes. Just an ordinary cup of tea, please.

**Louise** I'll make your tea.

**Simon** Where's Da?

**Margaret** Getting stuff from the car.

**Simon** Will I give him a hand?

**Margaret** Am I stopping you?

**Simon** No, Mama Bear, you are not, and I hope Goldilocks is in better temper.

**Margaret** Goldilocks – is that how you refer to your father?

**Simon** I'll stop calling him –

**Margaret** You will continue calling him Goldilocks. Especially when I am there. I know how much it will annoy him. Go out and give him a hand, Simon. He'll be all day.

*Simon goes out.*

What kind of form is he in – Simon?

**Louise** OK.

**Margaret** Has he come down here to blubber? Is that why you came down earlier than us? I want no weeping this weekend. That goes for all of us.

**Louise** Mother – we'll do as you command. Don't we always?

**Margaret** No, you don't, Louise. I'm afraid you don't.

**Louise** How is Da?

**Margaret** Saying nothing. Not one word. Weren't you listening to me? Saving all his shite jokes for the two of you. Breaking your hearts laughing. Jesus, your father – which is he worse as? *The Silent Woman* or *Bartholomew Fair*?

**Louise** What –

**Margaret** Plays by Ben Jonson. Fuck Ben Jonson. Too hard for students now. The effort of getting them to read him. Even the good ones.

**Louise** I thought you loved teaching Ben Jonson.

**Margaret** He's left me.

**Louise** Da?

*Louise pours tea.*

**Margaret** Ben Jonson. I just don't seem to have – to have the skill for it any more. I once had the energy that nothing daunted me, but now – let me forget about college this weekend. Louise, where is the tea?

**Louise** There you go –

*She hands her the tea.*
*Margaret tastes it.*

**Margaret** Grand – all right.

**Louise** Not perfect.

**Margaret** What?

**Louise** All right – grand. I'll have one myself.

*She pours herself a cup of tea and they drink in silence.*
*Leo and Simon enter the causeway.*
*Leo carries a suitcase and a black plastic bag full of food.*
*Simon carries another heavy rucksack.*

**Simon** Jesus, what has she packed in here?

**Leo** That woman carries the contents of the *Titanic* every time we come down here. I swear to Christ, she goes down diving through the cold Atlantic every time my back is turned.

**Simon** She can't even swim, Da.

**Leo** She probably threatens some poor merman to carry her on his back.

**Simon** How would you threaten a merman?

**Leo** With a very big fish-knife. She's had plenty of practice on me.

**Simon** Poor old ball-less fucker.

**Leo** I wouldn't bank on that, boyo. I could still fix you.

**Simon** Quit complaining.

*They enter the cottage.*

**Leo** I'll complain in my own house – which it is.

**Margaret** I might have some say in that.

**Leo** I'm sure you might. Here, now –

*He dumps down what he's carrying.*

Are you happy?

**Margaret** Happy – happy – would someone remind me of what that word means?

**Leo** Have you forgotten? Why's that? Have you Alzheimer's?

**Margaret** I might have. You could be landed with me dribbling at the mouth and peeing myself.

**Leo** You do that already – you've been doing it for years. So, I'll cope.

**Margaret** That's nice to know.

**Leo** Louise, is there any tea? Would you pour your father a cup?

**Margaret** I think there's only one cup left.

*She pours it into her own cup.*

I'm so sorry – were you gasping for a cup of tea? Well, you know where the tap is. Make it yourself. Or better still – have a long drink of water. Like yourself.

**Leo** How did I first fall for your mother?

**Simon** Looks?

**Margaret** Personality?

**Leo** No – it was her way of opening bottles with her breath.

**Margaret** You would know – you've opened a fair few in your pubs.

**Leo** I've never drunk the profits.

**Margaret** Something I've always admired – how careful with money you are. Some might even say miserly. In fact, isn't that your nickname? Mean – mean dog.

*She howls like a dog.*

**Leo** Who dares to call me that?

**Margaret** Me – your loving wife of many years standing.

**Leo** Aye, standing when you're sober enough.

**Margaret** I do my bit for the family business. I've never asked you for a free drink, and I've never been offered. Mean – mean dog.

**Louise** I'll make more tea.

**Simon** I'll help you.

**Margaret** How does it take two people to make a pot of tea?

**Leo** When one is more useless than the other.

**Margaret** You have them as you rear them.

**Louise** Sometimes you don't have them, even though you reared them. They're not there any more. Are they?

*Silence.*

Stop it now. Stop it immediately. I will not put up with this one minute longer.

**Leo** What are you talking about?

**Louise** Do you not know what I'm talking about? I think you do. I'm nipping this performance in the bud. Because it is all a pretence. I'm not playing, Da.

**Leo** Playing what?

**Louise** Pretending this is happy families. Don't dare do that. Don't dare act as if nothing's happened. As if nothing's changed. We can sit here and listen to the banter between our loud but loving parents. One word borrowing another, but sure it's all only our way – our way of saying nothing. I will no longer listen to that. I will not do it. That's my way of keeping the peace, Simon. I'm going out for a walk now. Down to the shore.

**Margaret** Louise, that's enough.

**Louise** Down to where my brother Gene died.

**Margaret** I said, enough.

**Louise** Dead at his own hand. He had downed every drop of alcohol he could find in this house. Consumed a fierce amount of alcohol. That's what the coroner's report says. I can hear his Galway voice.

*She mimics a Galway accent.*

A fierce amount of drink. A mountain of drink.

*She nearly breaks down as she returns to her own voice.*

He would not have known what he was doing –

**Margaret** I said I wanted no weeping this weekend. I'm going in for a rest, Leo, you do as you want.

*She goes into the bedroom, carrying a suitcase. Louise whispers.*

**Louise** You always run away, Ma.

**Simon** What in fuck brought that on?

**Louise** I wanted to be sure we know why we're here. He was sure what he was doing. To make sure he would die, my brother poisoned himself with drink and cut open his wrists. That's how he was found. Bled red. We assemble here in his name, to do what? Remember his death, or remember his birth? Twenty-one years ago he came into our world. Two years ago he left it. His choice. His way. His will. Neat and tidy. Everything neat and tidy.

*Leo's cup falls from his hand.*

Well done, Gene. You're shutting me up. But I don't believe you're listening. I'm not afraid of you.

**Simon** You're speaking out of turn, Loui. I think you're overtired. Do what Ma's doing. Go for a sleep.

**Leo** Do what your brother tells you –

**Louise** Which brother? I think the dead brother wants me to do what he tells me. Go for a walk down to where he died. All right, I will do as I am told – will we all do as he tells us, our dead brother, your dead son?

*She leaves the cottage.*

**Leo** Louise, don't stray too far. We might have a long hike later in the afternoon.

*She calls back, exiting.*

I'll do what you want, Da, whatever you want.

**Leo** So it's started.

**Simon** As it has to.

**Leo** We'll get through it, won't we?

*There is a fierce cry of seabirds.*
*Fade.*

# Act Two

*In the kitchen, Margaret prepares a chicken for cooking. It is already cut into pieces.*

*Simon peels potatoes.*

*On the table are two lemons, carrots, broccoli and a cauliflower.*

**Margaret** I presume you know better than I do – is that one still on medication?

**Simon** Louise – no, she gave it up six months ago. She's still seeing a counsellor now and again.

**Margaret** Grief counsellor?

**Simon** That's what they're called.

**Margaret** I gave up on them when I heard the racket one was doing with a medium, God forgive me saying the word. They were recommending each other to poor innocents. Then they'd exchange information and convince people they knew how to get through the mourning.

**Simon** Vultures.

**Margaret** I told you about the one waiting for me outside my office.

**Simon** You did.

**Margaret** Running up to tell me my son was happy – she'd been talking to him the night before. You can imagine my answer back to her.

**Simon** She deserved it, I'm sure.

**Margaret** A good day's hiking down that mountain will be good for the two of them.

*Simon hums 'Climb Every Mountain'.*

*The Sound of Music* – Julie Andrews warbling through the streets of Salzburg – watching it I knew why we invented the nuclear bomb.

**Simon** Jesus, poor Julie Andrews.

**Margaret** Fuck her. What did she ever do for Ireland?

**Simon** She's an Englishwoman.

**Margaret** I rest my case.

**Simon** How long till they're here?

**Margaret** When hunger hits them. They're like two goats, the way they can scale safely down that path. My heart was in my mouth the days I was trying it. I was always a mile behind them. You weren't much better than me. They never ever waited for us. Marching on ahead, regardless. Why are you saying nothing?

**Simon** Have I had a chance to say anything?

**Margaret** Who's stopping you?

**Simon** You've barely taken time to breathe.

**Margaret** Give my head peace. Have you enough spuds peeled?

**Simon** Not yet.

**Margaret** You would have thought I'd lose weight giving up drink. Not a sign of a difference. I'm eating more. Food tastes better. Do you find that?

**Simon** No, I don't drink in your house or in your company. Elsewhere, I do. So does Louise.

**Margaret** You never told me that, Simon.

**Simon** I didn't think I'd need to, so I'm telling you now. We all have our ways of coping. Sobriety – that's how you and Dad manage. I hand it to you – you've kept it up for nearly two years. I don't know how you do it.

**Margaret** I had to. I nearly had a breakdown. When I was lecturing one morning last year, I nearly went under. I did, in fact –

**Simon** You said nothing to me –

**Margaret** To no one. It only lasted one morning. I was in that big barn of a theatre – first year, five hundred students. There I was, pontificating to them about John Keats. And it dawned on me how young – so very young he was when he died –

**Simon** Jesus, Ma, that was close to the bone. Could someone else not have taught that?

**Margaret** I'd never realised how young – it never dawned on me until I had begun that lecture.

*She stops preparing the chicken.*
*She takes the potatoes Simon has peeled.*
*She washes them in a basin of cold water.*

I was saying the intensity of his letters – his late poems – and the letters are poetry in their own way – it was due to him dying, knowing he was dying too soon, a young man. When I said the words, I lost my voice. Lost it completely. Stopped speaking. The students twigged it. They knew about Gene, your brother. What they didn't know was I could see his face in every one of them. Boys, girls, my son's face. And I stood there, thinking, this is no good. Everything I've said this day, everything I've said in every lecture, it's no good. I'm no good. I just stood there seeing my child – my child repeated in row after row of students I'd let down. I could feel them panicking. I think they believed I was going to collapse. To die in front of them. I said you will have to excuse me. I am not well. This is pointless. All pointless. Keats – his poetry is all fear, fear of dying, dying young.

*The potatoes are all washed.*

I understand that now. I understand why he wrote,

'When I have fears that I may cease to be
Before my pen has glean'd my teeming brain –'

'My teeming brain –'

*Silence.*

What comes next?

**Simon**
'Before high-piled books in charactery
Hold like rich garners the full-ripen'd grain;
When I behold upon the night's starr'd face
Huge cloudy symbols of a high romance,
And think that I may never live to trace
Their shadows with the magic hand of chance;
And when I feel, fair creature of an hour,
That I shall never look at thee more –'

**Margaret** 'Never look upon thee more –' Yes, I remember. I stopped there. I told them – the lecture was over. I must have lasted no more than ten minutes – quarter of an hour. I don't recall how I got back to my office. Someone kind gave me a lift home. I was three days in bed. Sick as a dog. I really believed I'd never face another lecture again.

**Simon** But you did.

**Margaret** I faced it the following Monday. As if nothing happened. Quickly forgotten. That's the way we work in that department. All is buried and done for. Marked and corrected. The best way to work together. I did so. But it was close. Closer than I'd like to admit. For it was in public. Not smart, my lad.

**Simon** Why didn't you tell me?

**Margaret** I thought you might have had enough to deal with.

**Simon** Did Da know?

**Margaret** He believed what I told him. A heavy flu, that's what I had.

*She points to the lemon.*

Cut one lemon in half and slice the other.

*He does so.*

Give me the two halves.

*She squeezes the juice over the chicken.*
*She places the pieces in a roasting tin.*
*She squirts olive oil over the chicken.*
*Simon hands her the slices of lemon.*
*She places them over the chicken, together with some bay leaves.*

I wonder is your father going to leave me?

**Simon** Why would he do that?

**Margaret** I'm ancient. Well past childbearing. He's a rich old fool. Men are all eejits. They fall for young whores.

**Simon** Is he that rich?

**Margaret** If you stepped out of your bookshop job and went into his business you'd know there's plenty salted away. Maybe you do know that. Anyway, that's not the point. The first thing you should have pointed out is that I am not an ancient old cow.

**Simon** Who called you an ancient old cow?

**Margaret** I did. Just now. Contradict me.

**Simon** No.

**Margaret** Why not?

**Simon** I like cows.

**Margaret** Good for you.

**Simon** Good for me. How much is he worth anyway?

**Margaret** I'm not sure – a fair whack.

**Simon** What's a fair whack?

**Margaret** Simon, I know next to nothing about money. It's all fucking figures to me. I'm not great at numbers. We have enough. We have more than enough. We educated you and we could well have afforded you do doctorates, but you finish your master's and go to work in a bookshop. Louise does her degree and wants to teach primary school. That's what you want to do. Do it. But you are in a very lucky position, the two of you. If you each want to buy a house, we'll give you a deposit. You can afford to buy somewhere in Dublin. There are few your age in your choice of employment who can do that. That's how much –

**Simon** If Gene had lived, would you still be able to afford that?

**Margaret** Jesus, what kind of question is that?

*Silence.*

Is that all you think of your dead brother? Is that what you ask me? It is cruel, it is hurtful –

**Simon** Was he not the same? Cruel, hurtful, doing what he did?

**Margaret** When did this come into your head?

**Simon** When does it not? Are you telling me it never enters yours?

*Margaret fiercely prepares vegetables, segmenting broccoli, chopping carrots, dicing the cauliflower.*

**Margaret** Do you know what I'm going to tell you, sir?

**Simon** Tell me – do you not ever –

**Margaret** I tell you that beneath that lackadaisical manner you share one great fault with your father –

**Simon** What would that be, Mother?

**Margaret** Deeply – very deeply inside both – you two believe money is really all that matters. You don't have to worry about money, that's why you don't talk about it. You know how much you'll inherit. Why push yourself now when it's waiting for you later? Your da makes money – hand-over-fist money – he hoards money, more and more money. Where's it got him? He has no more learned what you have never thought of learning. It does not buy you everything, money. There are times when it's for fuck all. It can't –

**Simon** Bring back the dead. I never thought it could. Did he? Did you?

*Silence.*

How do you bring back the dead, Ma?

**Margaret** Work, Simon. I work – hard. What do you do, son?

**Simon** I let the dead stay buried.

**Margaret** That's sensible.

**Simon** And I'm still here.

**Margaret** So am I.

**Simon** Smart lady.

**Margaret** Smelly lady – that's what I am right now. Very smelly lady. A shower – that's what I need. You and Louise will be preening yourselves tonight. I need to use it now. That trickle of water takes an age to get clean under. I need to wash myself. Why did he not leave a note? Your brother –

**Simon** I don't know.

**Margaret** That might have made it a bit easier. What would he have said in it?

*Silence.*

'When I have fears that I may cease to be –'

**Simon** But he didn't have those fears.

**Margaret** I suppose he didn't. He had some kind of courage. That's some consolation. He wasn't afraid.

**Simon** Go in and take your shower, Ma.

**Margaret** Jesus, it's far from showers I was reared. I'll never forget when a neighbour got the first fridge in the town. We all trooped round to watch it open and close.

**Simon** It's a wonder you survived –

**Margaret** The Donegal winters?

**Simon** I was thinking more of the Donegal summers. What difference is there between –

**Margaret** The rain is warmer in summer. You don't tan – you rust. We don't need fancy swimming pools. We have roads. We can swim down them.

**Simon** You're very proud of your native county.

**Margaret** I am indeed – fiercely so.

**Simon** That's why you rarely go back?

**Margaret** It's home. Love it – leave it.

**Simon** When will I start cooking?

**Margaret** Now – they'll be back soon, hungry as wolves.

**Simon** Are we inviting cousin Bridget?

**Margaret** Bridget – I should, but Jesus, I don't think I can face her.

**Simon** The constant interrogation?

**Margaret** Yes. Maybe lunch tomorrow. Not tonight.

**Simon** On your own head be it.

*He places the chicken in the oven.*

**Margaret** Don't I know it.

*He places the pot of spuds on the cooker.*

Thanks, Simon – for the help – with the dinner.

**Simon** Of course – with the dinner.

*She eyes him carefully.*
*She exits to the shower.*
*Simon hums 'Climb Every Mountain'.*
*He finishes the vegetables.*
*During this Louise enters.*
*She throws herself onto one of the seats.*

**Louise** Jesus, my very arse is aching.

*Simon calls from the house.*

**Simon** Are you back?

**Louise** I said my arse is aching.

**Simon** There are people who pay good money for that kind of pleasure.

**Louise** I am not into that perversion. Yet. I'm gasping for a cold drink. Is there water in the fridge? Bring us out a glass.

*He pours water.*

**Simon** May I offer my commiserations and enquire about the sad passing of your late domestic servant?

**Louise** What?

**Simon** What did your last maid die of?

**Louise** Shut up, Simon. I'm in agony.

**Simon** Does Dad want one?

**Louise** He's not here. He went down to the beach.

*Silence.*

**Simon** He is all right?

**Louise** He's fine.

**Simon** I'll pour him some water.

**Louise** Where's Mum?

**Simon** She's having a shower.

*Simon comes out of the house with two glasses of water.*
*He gives one to Louise.*

Cheers.

**Louise** I wish it was something stronger.

**Simon** You know the rules.

**Louise** A beer would be nice.

**Simon** Lovely.

**Louise** Or a cider. I remember the lovely cider in Brittany. That summer I spent learning French in Lorient, the bottle frozen at your lips. I can smell the apples souring into sweet alcohol – a miracle.

*She sings.*

*Ces sont les filles de Lorient jolies,*
*Ces sont les filles de Lorient,*
*Mon dieu, qu'elles sont jolies, mon dieu,*
*Mon dieu, qu'elles sont jolies, lon-la.*

**Simon** You do need a drink.

**Louise** I know the rules.

*Leo enters.*

**Leo** I was having a look at that old currach abandoned on the shore.

**Simon** There's little left of it.

**Leo** The sea's eaten it away nearly. I'm sorry I didn't do what I'd once planned. Try to put it together again. We could have learned to use it. All of us.

**Louise** Can you see my mother setting foot on a currach?

**Leo** I was thinking of the boys. Three of us. I always think it mad to be surrounded by water and have no kind of boat. Would you have enjoyed it, Simon? Would he – Gene?

**Simon** I don't know.

**Leo** You never asked him – should we get a boat? He never said anything to you, did he? It's just dawned on me that if he knew how to sail, say, or just take a boat out into the water, he might have loved to do it.

**Louise** I don't think Ma would have let him, Daddy.

**Leo** He would not have had to tell her. He could have got up early. Even late at night, when we were asleep, he could have been alone, drifting through the darkness, calm, calming himself, away from us, in control of the boat. Would he have liked that, do you think?

**Simon** He might have.

**Leo** But you don't know. Neither do I. That's a new one, isn't it? Another excuse. If we'd had a boat, my son would have lived. Am I listening to myself? Am I going mad?

**Simon** I poured you a glass of iced water.

*Leo takes it and drinks.*

**Leo** How long is your mother going to keep us on an alcohol-free diet?

**Simon** You never break out –

**Louise** When she's not there?

**Leo** Alarmous Kate – your mother – the woman is always there, fretting.

**Simon** She told me today about the breakdown.

**Louise** What breakdown?

**Simon** Near breakdown – she passed it off as a bad flu. Did you know?

**Leo** I made a guess. I did nothing. She went back to work. We keep working. That's our way of coping. Might not be the best way, but so far – so far it's got us through.

**Louise** Which of the two of you wanted to come here for this?

**Leo** It was the two of us. We're glad you came with us.

**Simon** We wanted to come.

**Leo** Just for this year. His twenty-first. She's getting – getting more used – she's not bought a present. She still did up to last Christmas. I knew it was for him. A pair of shoes in his size. I confronted her. She said she'd forgotten he was dead. It slipped her mind when she was hassled shopping. I told her I didn't believe her. I said, Margaret, that's a lie. This carry-on has to stop, lady. And stop it has. There's no birthday presents. We'll just eat together tonight.

**Louise** Are we inviting Bridget?

**Simon** Herself says no – not tonight.

**Louise** She'll expect to be asked.

**Simon** She's not asked.

**Louise** She'll have a face on her.

**Leo** She can take it off her. We want nobody but ourselves tonight.

**Louise** She's just like a child, Da –

**Leo** Then you deal with her, teacher – it's what you do –

**Louise** I'd face fifty crying kids rather than one hell-bent Bridget –

**Simon** You were her favourite when we were youngsters.

**Louise** Face it – I was nobody's favourite. You were always the prodigy and were going to write masterpieces. Gene was great at maths and science. Muggins here was the eejit stuck in the middle, going to end up –

**Leo** Would you like to buy a house?

*Silence.*

Each of you, a house – money down, no mortgage?

**Simon** You're talking a fortune.

**Leo** Maybe so. I've my finger in a fair few pubs. The Irish drink. We're pissing our prosperity into the wind. They're lining my pockets nicely. It's all honestly got. It's natural I should share it with my children. Fuck waiting till I'm dead. No pockets in the shroud.

**Simon** Have you run this by Mother?

**Leo** How can she stop me giving you what's going to be yours? How is either of you going to get a deposit –

**Louise** By our own efforts – me teaching kids, him selling books –

**Leo** You've done what you want to do. I've not stood in your way. I don't need to. I know what's going to happen when it comes to the crunch. The two of you will take over the business.

**Louise** I don't think so –

**Leo** I do. You know why – your mother. Do you imagine that hard-headed Donegal woman will let a goldmine slip through our fingers? I doubt it. So do you. Where is she anyway?

**Simon** She went in for a shower a while ago.

**Leo** That was a nice climb, wasn't it, pet?

**Louise** It was not, Da, no.

*Margaret enters the kitchen.*
*Silence.*

**Leo** You didn't enjoy it?

**Louise** I really missed Gene.

*Silence.*

**Simon** He loved the mountain.

*Silence.*

That's why he died here.

**Leo** We do know that, Simon. Keep your mouth shut.

**Simon** We're not supposed to mention it still? Jesus, isn't this why we came here this weekend? Are we going to be allowed to remember him, me and Louise? Or are you and Ma going to be the sole mourners?

*Margaret enters the causeway.*

**Margaret** How have we put a stop to your mourning?

**Louise** As you never tire to remind us, we're in your house. In there your rules reign.

**Margaret** And you know why? They work.

**Simon** Ma, sometimes it might be better –

**Margaret** We give way? We give in? We start to wonder out loud why he did it? Sorry, no, Simon, not my way. Do the wondering elsewhere.

*Silence.*
*She sits on a seat.*

I've had my shower. I've left enough water. Your da will surely be a gentleman and let the lady refresh herself. Louise, do you stink after your physical exertions?

**Louise** A lady never stinks, Mama. My very farts are perfume.

**Margaret** Really? I wish you'd told me that when I was cleaning your ass as an infant. You weren't much better, my big son.

*She pulls Simon onto her knee and ruffles his hair.*

Don't cross your old mother. Her bark is worse than her bite.

*She kisses his hand.*

**Louise** I see a visitor approaching.

*Margaret and Simon stand.*

**Margaret** Bridget? What is she pushing in front of her?

**Louise** A child's buggy. She found it somewhere. She's using it as a walking frame.

**Margaret** Is she getting shaky on her pins?

**Louise** Compliment her on it. She thinks it's great.

**Simon** Wait for the pressure to be asked tonight. Are you going to relent, Ma?

**Margaret** I'll ask her to lunch tomorrow before we leave.

**Louise** How are you going to fend her off?

**Margaret** By saying nothing. The rest of you, do the same.

**Leo** You're a brave woman if you succeed.

*Bridget enters wheeling the buggy.*

Here comes the stranger. How are you, cousin?

**Margaret** I was about to call up to see you.

**Louise** I told her you'd been down to see if they'd arrived –

**Bridget** That was hours ago. Not a sign of you since then. I remembered the old saying. If the mountain won't go to the mountain, then Mohammed must go to Mohammed. What in Jesus does that mean? Has it something to do with cooking? Now that's a lovely smell from the kitchen. What is it?

**Simon** It is chicken, Bridget.

**Bridget** Dear me, very swanky, chicken and it not even Christmas, so Louise reminded me. Do you know, I would not thank you for chicken. I would not thank you.

**Margaret** Why is that, Bridget?

**Bridget** They're disgusting. Rolling in the muck, grunting, the smell of their dung would knock you down. Some people won't touch their flesh for religious reasons. I've heard tell of one eating an infant –

**Leo** That's pigs, woman.

**Bridget** In these parts, it's chicken. Revolting. What are you having with it?

**Simon** Potatoes.

**Bridget** My God, no. Very unlucky. I wouldn't put a potato in my mouth. Do you know that years ago – centuries ago – around here people were poisoned eating potatoes? They were lying by the side of the road foaming at the mouth, seeing things from too much of the accursed vegetable. They had a name for it –

**Louise** The Famine – the Irish Famine?

**Bridget** How in fuck was it a Famine? They were eating spuds like savages. No, if I remember correctly, it was called the Feed. The Dirty Feed. Do you know what I'm going to tell you? Ireland never recovered from it. The potato. Filthy creatures. Have you ever tasted snake?

**Margaret** I haven't.

**Bridget** Neither have I. Wasn't St Patrick a gobshite to expel them from this country? What harm were they doing? Rearing their young – minding their own business – doing their best – scaring the shite out of priests and bishops. Why didn't the bollocks show chickens the road instead of the snakes?

**Margaret** Maybe he liked the bit –

**Bridget** Of chicken? What's wrong with you, woman? St Patrick would only eat weeds and flowers. Where do you think he got the attachment to the shamrock? He was a dreadful man for roses, daffodils, a little dish of daisies, bluebells, buttercups. He could go through a bunch of fuchsia in a single sitting. Come winter the poor man fasted. He had to. But he could of course talk to birds. So can I. They don't listen. They sing and tell you to piss off. Lonely – it is, terrible to be lonely, talking to birds. Pitying snakes. Putting flowers at your door for bastarding St Patrick. What are you having for your sweet?

**Margaret** Cake.

**Bridget** Cake – of course. For his birthday. Your dead son's. Gene. Poor Eugene.

*Silence.*

I can still see him.

**Louise** So can we all, Bridget.

**Bridget** But I found him. He was all cold. He was red. You must miss him.

*Silence.*

You never know the day nor hour.

**Leo** No, you don't.

**Bridget** Why do you think he did it?

**Margaret** If we could answer that, Bridget, maybe he might not have done it.

**Bridget** Very wise, Margaret. What kind of cake is it?

**Margaret** Lemon cake – his favourite. Don't tell me you've something against lemons?

**Bridget** A sour taste. They leave your mouth numb. His lips were numb. I tried to rub life into them. I did try to get him breathing. But he was dead. The ambulance men said I could have done nothing. Nothing whatsoever.

**Simon** We do know that, Bridget.

**Bridget** If one of you smart young ones – even you, Margaret – if you had been a doctor –

**Margaret** None of us are doctors, Bridget –

**Bridget** You might have saved him, if you had been. Why didn't you become a doctor?

**Leo** Because we were like yourself, Bridget – too stupid.

**Louise** We didn't get into medicine.

**Bridget** Then you should have done what I do. Insist. Simply insist. No, I won't have a slice of cake. I know how generous you are and you'll offer. It would sit like a rock in my stomach. Lovely smell, lemons. Pity about the taste. Do you think it's lucky to have lemon cake at a birthday?

**Louise** What would you want at yours?

**Bridget** An old woman like me doesn't need birthdays. She should be looking forward to her funeral. Do you know what I'd like served at mine? Trifle – sherry trifle.

**Margaret** You like sherry trifle?

**Bridget** I fucking hate it. And I hope it chokes the lot of them. Why should they be enjoying themselves when I'm lying dead? If anyone feels pleasure at my wake, I swear I'll come back and haunt them. They can, you know, come back – the dead. If they want to. You can't bring them back just because you miss them or you want them back, or you have money. No amount of money can bring back the dead, no amount of making it. That's a valuable lesson. Don't forget it. I won't eat with you tonight. This should be a family occasion. Have a close family occasion. I'll leave you and love you and I'll close with a song. This is an old one we used to sing in these wild parts to cheer ourselves up.

*She starts to sing and do a crazy dance.*
*Margaret joins in the song.*
*Leo starts to dance with Bridget.*

She's a little crazy,
People say she's lazy,
And her life's a mystery,
But love grows where my Rosemary goes
And nobody knows like me.

I'm a lucky fella,
And I just gotta tell her
That I love her endlessly,
For love grows where my Rosemary goes
And nobody knows like me.

*She stops, breathless.*

I love that one. I used to dance the feet off myself. It was all the rage. Weddings, christenings, birthdays. Are you giving presents? No, you wouldn't be. It's not Christmas. Still and all, I have something for you.

*Out of the buggy she takes a letter.*

I thought I would save this for when nobody else was about. Just ourselves. I wanted to keep it until you were over the big shock. You know what it is, don't you?

*Silence.*

I found it – in his coat pocket.

*She leaves it on the seat.*

I hope you're not angry with me, keeping it secret till now. I just think this is the right time. You can see now why I'm not asking to stay. I would hate to intrude, even if you were going to ask me.

*She starts to wheel the buggy, stops, looks back at them.*

He's glad to be gone. Don't cry tonight. He would not like that. I should know. I cradled him in my arms. I comforted him. He was like my baby. My beautiful baby. Silent – not crying – in my arms.

*She sings as she exits.*

There came a gypsy riding – riding – riding –
Riding here to marry – to marry – marry –

*They stand, shell-shocked.*

**Simon** What the hell made her do that?

**Louise** I know she's a bit touched, but that was –

**Simon** How could she have kept that back from –

**Louise** Did she know what she was doing? Is she mad –

**Margaret** Mad as a fox. She knew what she was doing. Badness, a bad bitch. She knows how to hurt us. She didn't want to see the harm done. It was enough to pull the letter out. Enough to see our faces. It was as if she'd found him again, but we were here this time to see it.

**Simon** Why are you saying nothing, Da?

**Leo** I'm not sure why she did that to us.

*Silence.*

I would like to see the letter. Open it and read what it says.

**Margaret** No. We will do no such thing. We will carry it inside our house. We will read it in our own good time. Look, I can see her watching us. I will not allow her to witness how we receive this letter. I have a meal arranged for tonight. It is my son's birthday. His twenty-first. And my dead son, in his way, has left a gift to be delivered to us. Thank you, Bridget, for doing so. We will open it as we have always opened gifts. After we have lit and blown out the candles on the cake. We will do things as we've always done. We have to. That is the only way I know how to deal with this – this. He left a note. He did leave a note. How could she hold it back from me – his mother?

*She nearly cracks, but recovers.*

Am I wrong in asking we wait to read this?

**Simon** I'll do what you want, Ma.

**Louise** Whatever pleases you and Da.

**Margaret** What do you say, Leo?

**Leo** Is anybody else starving?

**Louise** Is the dinner ready?

**Simon** Very nearly.

**Louise** Then we'll get on with it. Come on, I'll give you a hand. Don't worry – I'm not going to poison you. I can set the table and serve.

*Louise and Simon go in to prepare dinner.*

**Leo** You can tear it up, you know. Throw it away – into the sea. Bury it on the beach where they found his body.

**Margaret** Was he a coward?

*Silence.*

Why did he do it?

**Leo** It might tell us, the letter.

**Margaret** Will we read it –

**Leo** When we're ready.

**Margaret** Yes.

**Leo** Come in – we'll eat soon.

**Margaret** Go in to them. Comfort them. Give them time to prepare. That's why I hold back reading it. You have to make them understand that. Go in to them.

*Leo enters the house.*

**Louise** Water, Da?

**Leo** Jesus, what I'd give for a large whiskey.

**Simon** We know.

**Louise** Would you like some Fanta?

**Leo** Fuck Fanta. Double-fuck Fanta.

**Simon** Da, fetch Ma inside.

*Leo goes back to the garden.*
*Margaret is still standing, listening in silence.*

**Margaret**
'Thou wast not born for death, immortal bird.'

**Leo** Who are you talking to?

**Margaret** Nightingale. Keats – his 'Ode to a Nightingale'. He calls it 'immortal bird'.

**Leo** You'll not hear much of them in these parts.

**Margaret** I've never heard an actual nightingale – only recordings. I never knew what's the fuss. Maybe they sound better out in the fields. My grandmother worked on a farm. A big, strong woman – she could do anything a man could do, even the sorest work. Would I have been better off if I'd never read a book? Stuck to where I belong down in the dirty clay, roughing it with the rest of my breed? Answer me that.

**Leo** I know better.

**Margaret** I asked Eugene that once. He told me I would have been happier if I'd stayed put. He didn't tell me why, though. Maybe he'll tell me in this.

*She looks at the letter.*

'Now, more than ever, seems it rich to die,
To cease upon the midnight –'

**Leo** Are you back talking to that fucking nightingale? Will you get in here to the house? If Bridget finds out you've gone with the birds in this garden, she'll call the police. Hasn't she done enough harm for one evening?

**Margaret** We'll see.

*She looks at the letter.*

We'll have patience and we'll see.

*She puts the letter into her pocket.*
*Fade.*

# Act Three

*Night.*

*After the meal.*

*The table has been cleared.*

*There are bottles of soft drinks, juices and mineral water around the kitchen.*

*The birthday cake has been cut.*

*Margaret toys with a slice, cutting it smaller and smaller.*

*Leo does not eat his.*

*Simon and Louise eat their cake.*

**Louise** Does anyone mind if I help myself to another bit of cake?

**Leo** I'm not a great man for the sweet things. You know that. Have this, you.

**Louise** Are you not mad about it either, Ma? You've barely –

**Margaret** Louise, pet, would you just stuff your face and not watch me –

**Louise** It's hard not to –

**Margaret** In my good time I will open the letter.

**Simon** Jesus, Ma, why won't you open it?

*Silence.*

If you can't, will you let one of us do it? Sitting here –

**Margaret** There is nothing to stop you leaving, Simon. Get into the car. Drive up to the pub. The three of you, go on. Douse yourself with drink. It's what you want to do. Don't let me stop you.

**Simon** If we did, would you come with us?

**Margaret** Then we can crawl back here, reeking of drink, open another bottle and have a good old cry together, recalling our beloved Gene, sweet, soft boy, too beautiful to live. Would that be the plan? I'll pass. You may be in the mood for carousing, but me –

**Leo** You – what kind of mood are you in?

**Margaret** I don't know. Don't want to know.

**Leo** Know what?

**Margaret** What's in this letter. I cannot face it.

**Leo** You have to.

*Silence.*

**Louise** Six months ago or so, an autistic child was sent to my class to see if she could be taught with ordinary kids. The girl was beautiful. Golden hair. Magnificent eyes. From the minute she arrived, she began to scream. She never stopped the entire morning. And I hear her again right now. That bloody letter pains me the way that child does. Put me out of my misery. Read what he says or else tear it to bits.

**Leo** One thing's always puzzled me. Who gave him the load of cash he had on him? Was it one of you?

*Louise and Simon shake their heads.*

**Margaret** I know where he got the money from. He had four hundred euro in his pocket. Nobody knew where he got that amount from. I did know, but I told nobody.

**Leo** Where did he get it?

**Margaret** Me.

**Louise** Ma, you're a mean Donegal bitch, no soft touch –

**Margaret** He stole it from me. Eugene thieved it –

**Leo** You never have that big a sum –

**Margaret** I kept foreign currency in a certain book. He knew that, he'd seen me do it. He started to take it and change into Irish money. I knew he was thieving. Eugene was a thief.

**Leo** How much was he stealing?

**Margaret** As much as I could afford.

**Louise** You gave him –

**Margaret** He took what I left him.

**Simon** Why did you –

**Margaret** Aid and abet my thief of a son? To stop him stealing outside the house. I knew the word for it is 'enabling'. I prefer to call myself a coward. A frightened woman watching her son get worse, not able to talk to him, not able to do anything, hoping the rest of her family are noticing something is not right – hoping her husband, her older son, her daughter –

**Simon** We did not give him money.

**Margaret** Well, bully for you – aren't you great? Big pats on the back for all of you. It's all down to my fault. The Bank of Ireland here dished out the dough and now she reaps her reward. My son is dead and it's due to me.

**Leo** Do you know what you're doing now, Margaret?

**Margaret** I'm sure you'll tell me, Leo.

**Leo** I think in some way you're showing off. You're acting the martyr. How often have I listened to that tune? If I had a penny for every time –

**Margaret** – you heard it, you would be a rich man. But you are a rich man, a very rich man. Well done. What a pity bad comes with good. You put a child into the grave before you go into it. A grown child waiting for you, for me – I wonder what he'll say to us.

**Leo** Do you think I've not asked myself –

**Margaret** He will turn his face away from you. Away from all of us. Do you know why? This will tell us why.

*She tears open the letter.*
*She reads it.*

**Louise** What does he say?

*Margaret hands Louise the letter.*
*Louise reads it.*

**Margaret** Tell them.

*Silence.*

Tell them what's in the letter.

*Silence.*

Are you struck dumb? Tell them.

**Louise** He gives his own name. His date of birth. The day he died. Then he gives your name, Da. Ma's name. Your name, Simon. And my name.

**Simon** That's it?

**Louise** That's it.

**Simon** That's all?

**Louise** All.

**Simon** Nothing else but his name – and our names?

**Margaret** You're forgetting something.

**Simon** What?

**Margaret** His date of birth, and the date he died. He knew so what he was doing. He wanted to die. At least we now know. He did want to die.

**Leo** That is answered.

**Margaret** It's answered all right.

**Louise** Bridget will be broken-hearted. Nothing to tell her.

**Simon** He said nothing.

**Margaret** I think he said plenty. I think he said everything he wanted to say to us.

**Louise** He just said his name.

**Simon** And our names.

**Margaret** What do you make of that, Leo? How do you read that?

**Leo** I leave the reading to you.

**Margaret** But I'm asking you – how should I read this?

**Leo** I'm not sure I want to know, Margaret.

**Margaret** I think you need to know. Isn't it a pity we didn't invite Bridget tonight? That wise old madwoman could read this clear as daylight. No, she wouldn't need to. She could see through the envelope. She made out what he was telling us – what he was doing to us. And she passed on his message when the time was right.

**Simon** What are you saying his message is, Ma?

**Margaret** His date of birth. His death day. His name, our names. We're born – we die. The curse of Adam. Your brother reminds us. He curses us.

**Louise** You should have left that superstition behind you in Donegal. There's no such thing –

**Margaret** What do you think, Leo? Do you believe me? Have I not always read for you – the signs, the secrets, good luck and bad luck – have I not always been worth listening to? Have I not given you excellent advice? Was that just nonsense, just Donegal superstition? Am I right? Is your dead son putting us under his curse?

**Leo** You must lift that curse.

**Margaret** I can't.

**Leo** Then what are we going to do?

**Simon** We take no notice –

**Louise** I'm with Simon on this.

**Margaret** Simon, why have you decided not to have kids?

*Silence.*

Haven't you made up your mind – no children?

**Simon** Who told you?

**Margaret** Your dead brother, darling. It's his gift to you in death. You're frightened of having any children because of him.

*Silence.*

**Leo** Is that true, son?

**Margaret** Is it?

**Simon** If I don't want kids, Ma, maybe that's down to me. Maybe it's more to do with you than with Gene.

**Margaret** You'd need to explain yourself there.

**Simon** I choose not to.

**Margaret** You cannot say what you've said to me –

**Simon** I can say what I like to you –

**Margaret** I'm glad to hear it – so elaborate for me –

**Simon** Elaborate – explain – analyse – consider – discuss – illustrate – refer to at least two texts on your course – piss off, Mother. We're not in one of your seminars.

**Margaret** That is not fair –

**Simon** If I want to keep my mouth shut –

**Margaret** Why do you not want a child?

**Simon** Because I would fail. I would fail as a father. And you would waste no time letting me know it. Coaching me, advising me, warning me – letting me bask in your wisdom. Why are you so wise a parent? Why do you know best? It's actually because of your great loss. Your son has died. You've suffered the worst. You've survived it. And that makes you – what does it make you, Mother? Perfect. And fuck you for being so perfect. Louise is here to speak for herself. But may I say on behalf of myself, on behalf of Eugene, fuck you for being – being –

**Margaret** Perfect. That was your word. I make no apologies for that. It's what has me where I am and what I've made of myself. I have rules and I stick to them. I've needed to. You know where I come from. The back of beyond –

**Louise** Not the Donegal lament. The first one from your council estate to go to college. Living on handouts from the county council and your poor parents who could afford to give you next to nothing. Having to win scholarships to finish off your course. Struggling with Da to pay rent and put food –

**Leo** Stop this mockery –

**Louise** That's history, Da, not mockery. We don't mock –

**Leo** Nor should you. It's the truth you're laughing at –

**Margaret** Let her laugh. It's what they should do, the young against the old. Instil that into them. A good laugh. Maybe if we'd let him laugh louder at us, we would not be mourning Gene. But we are. Though Louise wants to laugh. Here's another laugh. Feel my hands – feel them.

*Margaret grabs Louise's hands into her own.*

Are they soft? No, they're rough. They're like sandpaper. How did I get them reading books and marking papers? I'd love you to be able to tell me, because I don't know myself. Maybe it's just in my bones. I can't be the genteel type. Maybe it's because I clawed my way into that job at the university and my hands are indeed claws. Laugh at this, lady. When I was asked at my interview, did I intend to start a family, I could honestly answer, no, for I'd started well before. I make a point of bringing all three of you into my office on my first day. Jesus, the look on their faces – you'd think I'd given birth on the corridor. Have a good laugh at that. I paid a tough price to be a teacher. I will let nothing and nobody deny me that. When I was a young one, I made my vow to each of you. I would not stand before any of you as adults and tell you you stopped me doing what I wanted. I have kept that vow.

*She turns to Simon.*

I have kept that vow perfectly.

**Louise** Has he cursed me as well? How has he cursed me?

*Silence.*

Does he curse me with a question? Does he ask me a question? Why was it him and not me who did it?

**Simon** Ma, look what you started – all this talk about curses –

**Margaret** That we all still believe. There's a lump of the peasant very deep inside you, Louise. I don't believe you'd do what you say you might have done, daughter. You belong to the soil. You won't defile it. But I can't answer your question. You'll have to do that.

**Leo** Do it soon. That's the way madness works. Asking questions – always asking. Enough to drive anybody off their head. Drive them daft.

**Louise** I have thought about it before. Thought about it since. When did he decide to die, going through what townland or parish? Somebody must have given him a lift here. Did he tell them what he was going to do? Nobody's come forward to say they saw him on the road. Do they not want to get involved? He's left me all those questions. Do they stop me doing it myself?

**Simon** No, they don't. You don't want to kill yourself. He did. That's what the note proves. You're different from him.

**Margaret** Where was all the money going? For once, I want a straight answer. Tell me what you know.

**Simon** He was drinking hard.

**Louise** He was gambling.

**Simon** The boy had the makings of an addict.

**Louise** If it wasn't going to the drink, it would be the harder stuff.

**Simon** If it wasn't cocaine, it would have been the gee-gees.

**Louise** It would have been a mixture of all three. Who knows what he's been spared? Thanks, Eugene. The biggest favour you did this family was your suicide. You've certainly saved me the bother of attempting it. One victim is enough. Fuck off now. Is that right, Ma? Stand up to the bastard, send him back to the spirit world with a ringing in his ears? This is how your family deal with your ghosts – bog on back –

**Margaret** To where? Back to where?

*Silence.*

Leo, what did you ask me to do about the curse?

**Leo** I asked you to lift it.

**Margaret** What did I answer?

**Leo** You said you can't. I asked then what we'd do.

**Margaret** Should we make a start by doing this?

*She tears the envelope in half.*

And the next thing we do is this.

*She tears the sheet of notepaper.*

Just to make sure we'll do this.

*She tears the envelope and notepaper together.*

And I'd say we'd all feel this is right to continue.

*She gathers all the pieces together.*

Let's go outside into the darkening light.

*She goes out of the house.*
*They follow her.*

Now, Gene, should you be watching us, this is what we do, as we did with your ashes, we scatter your last will and testament into the air. Dispose of these, your final written words, as you desire.

*She throws pieces of paper into the wind.*

Confetti, darling, not for your wedding but for your burial, your last resting place, as is fitting, for my son – you loved death, you married her, and so she took your life. I never thought this would be the ceremony that would separate you from your mother. On this day you were born – could I have imagined you would lead me to this corner of the west of Ireland where I would reveal your great secret to the winds? What is this secret? You were born for death, my mortal child.

*She scatters the remains of the paper.*

We are all born for death, my fragile flesh, my living babies. Your brother does more than remind us of that. He recommends it. It is his preferred way of existing. And he urges me – he urges his mother – to play his game – to join in the fun – to follow my leader.

*She sings.*

Following my leader – my leader – my leader –
Following my leader wherever he may go.

*She stops singing.*

What's wrong with you? Is nobody going to join in?

*Leo sings, taking her by the arm.*

**Leo**
Following my leader – my leader – my leader –
Following my leader wherever he may go.

*He tries to steer her into the house.*

*She resists gently, stopping singing, letting go of his arm.*

**Margaret** No – not a chance – I'm not going back in there yet. I've something to do.

**Simon** What can you have to do?

**Louise** It's too late for visiting –

**Margaret** Visiting – that's it –

**Louise** Bridget is no night-owl –

**Margaret** Owls – that's it – that's who I need to talk to. And ravens – the nightingale – all the birds of the air. They'll tell me what to do. I've been mad living in this part of the earth, and I've never known or listened to those creatures –

**Simon** Da, you have to do something.

**Leo** Listen to her. Let her speak.

**Louise** She's making no sense.

**Margaret** Excuse me, I am always talking sense. It is my misfortune. You may think differently. All of you. You may see sitting on my shoulder a dead weight. You are wrong. It is a child perched there. My son. He is like a bird. A raven. An owl.

**Leo** A nightingale?

**Margaret** No, Leo, wrong there – not a nightingale.

**Leo** What happened to him?

**Margaret** The nightingale's dead. The boy who sang baby songs, the child who loved poetry, the young fellow great at sums, my gold, my happiness, my hope – Jesus, he is dead. My son is dead. He took his own life. I demand to know why. I want the rocks on the shore – the sea in the ocean – answer me why. I want the ground – the earth – the mountains tell me why. I want the birds of the air to explain. Why is he not living? Why is he no more?

**Louise** Mammy, I want you back. I want it now.

**Margaret** I never leave you. What makes you think I'd leave you? The three of you and your daddy. Sure, you're the world to me. I have to work hard to look after you. So does your father. You must get the best. Better than I got. You see, I cheated. I lied to get the job. I said I have no children. And it's brought me bad luck. It's why I lost Gene. He's very angry with me.

**Louise** He's dead, Ma, dead and gone.

**Simon** We're here. We want you to come back to us.

**Margaret** I haven't gone away. I haven't gone anywhere. What's wrong with them? Why are they asking me this, Leo? Give them a slap.

**Leo** We do not raise our hand against our children.

**Margaret** Give them a hiding. Give them what was done to me if I crossed my father or my mother. The hand across my face. The belt across my arse. Belt across my face. The cane against my cunt. If you do that to me again, I'm going to kill myself. I'm going to kill myself.

*Leo takes her in his arms.*
*She calms down.*

I'm going to kill myself.

**Leo** You didn't.

**Margaret** I'm going to kill my father.

**Leo** He's dead now and he's buried. As Gene is. You've got over your father. You're getting over Gene.

**Margaret** And I've kept my job?

**Leo** No better woman to hold down her job.

**Margaret** The other two – the wains –

**Leo** They're here. Worried about you –

**Margaret** Simon?

**Simon** Present and correct, Mother.

**Margaret** Louise?

**Louise** Not yet, Ma – don't think it's finished yet.

**Simon** Louise, give her –

**Louise** We'll finish this tonight. The curse, Ma – his curse – what did he want of you and Daddy?

*Silence.*

Come on, you say you can read what he's actually saying. What was the curse on you and Da?

*Silence.*

**Margaret** It would be nice, wouldn't it, to walk into the water? Together, all of us.

**Leo** Go for a paddle.

**Margaret** No, not a paddle. A swim.

**Leo** At this hour of the night?

**Margaret** We could go to him, you know.

**Leo** But we're not going to.

**Margaret** Are you sure?

**Leo** I insist we're not, Margaret.

**Margaret** Then what you say goes.

**Leo** Occasionally. Very occasionally.

**Margaret** He does want us.

**Louise** You heard – we're not going. None of us.

**Margaret** You're very hard, Louise. I can hear him crying.

**Louise** I can hear him laughing. That's why I've lost pity.

**Simon** He's lost his life, Louise.

**Louise** He took his life, Simon. There's a difference. I know that now. So should you.

**Margaret** Was I mad out here earlier?

**Leo** You were grand. Wasn't she?

**Louise** Grand.

**Simon** The best.

**Margaret** I have the distinct impression I was mad.

**Leo** I've seen you worse.

**Margaret** When?

**Leo** After four bottles of red wine.

**Margaret** I have never in my entire life drank four bottles –

**Leo** Your cousin Joe's wedding.

**Margaret** That was in Sligo, for fuck's sake. I had to get through it someway. Jesus Christ, do you know I'm wrecked.

**Louise** Come with me, beddy-byes for us. We'll leave the men to the moonlight.

**Margaret** Right. Early enough start. Bridget wants her lunch. Forgive her and feed her.

*She rises to go into the house.*
*Louise goes with her.*

You boys, don't be too late. It's not that warm. If you don't watch yourselves, you'll get a foundering.

**Simon** Foundering?

**Margaret** Donegal word. Did I never use it to you? It means cold – chill – frozen. It's how we refer to Dublin people. The foundered. Nighty-nighty.

**Louise** See you in the morning.

**Margaret** Aye – the morning.

*They go into the house.*
*Leo and Simon sit looking at each other.*

**Louise** Do you want a cup of tea before you hit the hay?

**Margaret** I'd like that.

**Louise** Will I make it weak?

**Margaret** No, I can take strong. I'll sleep tonight.

*Louise makes tea.*

**Leo** Do you know what I'm going to say, son, and I want you to remember this very clearly.

**Simon** I will remember, Da.

**Leo** Can you imagine this night if there had been drink involved?

**Simon** I don't suppose –

**Leo** I've come prepared for all emergencies?

**Simon** Have you?

**Leo** Back of the car. Half a bottle of Power's whiskey and a few Guinness. Fetch them, like a good young fella. They're hiding in my tool box.

**Simon** Tool box? You've never changed a lightbulb –

**Leo** I'm learning. Keep your voice down. Go on, do what your da tells you.

*Louise gives Margaret the cup of tea.*
*Simon exits.*
*Leo sits alone.*
*A blast of wave showers him.*

It's all right – I'm here.

**Louise** Do you know what I think we should do tomorrow?

**Leo** I know you're lonely.

**Louise** We should go down to the beach.

**Margaret** And see where –

**Louise** – he was found, yes.

**Leo** I've not talked to you tonight.

**Margaret** Yes, I'll do it, but put no pressure on anyone.

**Leo** I will tomorrow.

**Margaret** Go up to your bed, Louise. I'm grand.

**Louise** Are you sure?

**Margaret** Yes.

*Louise climbs up to her loft bed.*
*Margaret sits alone in the kitchen.*

**Leo** Mammy had to talk tonight. I will tomorrow, darling. I will tomorrow. Bridget will be here. Your old pal. She'll help me. Have patience.

*The swell of the sea.*
*Fade.*

# Act Four

*The morning after.*
*Leo sits with Bridget in the kitchen.*
*Bridget eats a slice of cake.*
*Margaret, Louise and Simon are on the beach.*

**Bridget** I'm still sorry to miss Margaret.

**Leo** You haven't – they're gone for a walk on the shore. Do you like the lemon cake?

**Bridget** I didn't, no, but I'll take this last slice. Pity to waste it. Do you see this cake? That is my champagne. I never drink. Never touch a drop. Gin, whiskey, vodka, rum, beer, brandy, wine, porter – they all disagreed with me.

**Leo** You tried them all?

**Bridget** Many times. I might be found lying stocious under a tree, singing, 'I see the moon, the moon see me.' I gave it up when the tree started to join in the song. Do you think, does the moon see us? I wonder in what way it sees us? I'd love to know. Do you know what I think you should do? Sell this house. He won't go uncared for. Not while I'm here.

**Leo** You gave us all a bad fright – the letter.

**Bridget** It must have been shocking, but don't thank me.

**Leo** For what?

**Bridget** My kindness in keeping it from you, till you were ready to receive it.

**Leo** Were we ready?

**Bridget** You are now. You're over it. That's why you can sell.

**Leo** You've very keen to be rid of your nearest and dearest.

**Bridget** We're only distant cousins.

**Leo** You were a great help when we were first buying.

**Bridget** The least I could do for my own, even if we're at a far remove.

**Leo** Are we that bad neighbours?

**Bridget** You've been the best, but you're bad luck. You're very kind people, but no harm to you, it would have been better if you never came here. You're decent as any creature ever looked over a half-door, but, Jesus, do you get notions. You don't belong here. Fuck off.

**Leo** Ireland of the welcomes, you'll never die.

**Bridget** What would I be doing welcoming anybody? Nobody asked you to come here. You barely land but you're off again. I have to laugh at how you expect me to mourn your dead son. He was a nice enough boy, but I've no more tears. I've cried my eyes out years ago over another death. A very sad death.

**Leo** Whose?

**Bridget** My own. It was a lovely funeral, though I say so myself. I also have to confess I was quite vexed none of you attended.

**Leo** Because it never happened. You're not dead.

**Bridget** You're right there. I can't argue with that. But you do know what I'm talking about. Dying before your time. You've done it yourself, haven't you? Putting your child in the earth? That's like dying, isn't it?

**Leo** Yes.

**Bridget** Worse than dying, isn't it?

**Leo** I can't say – I've never died.

**Bridget** But you can guess.

**Leo** I can guess.

**Bridget** What's it like?

**Leo** Worse than dying.

*Silence.*

You have to go on living. Night after night – day after day – breath after breath. I started to hear myself breathing. I wanted it to stop. Just stop. I couldn't do that.

*Silence.*

I've never thought my son a coward, because whatever else it took to drive him to do what he did with his life, he had courage – great courage – that I lacked to copy him, Bridget. And I wanted to –

**Bridget** Did you?

**Leo** There were times I wanted to.

**Bridget** We've all wanted to. We've all thought of it. What's in store for me? A lonely old woman, pushing anyone near her far away. Sell the house – do you know why? I don't want to let you see what's coming to me. More mad, more malignant, more danger to myself. Maybe my reason will be maimed and my mind shattered, me sitting helpless in a hospital starving, dying of thirst – no family to give a tinker's curse if I live or let go. Jesus, is suicide not better than that fate? If it is, I still don't have the courage to commit it. I too am a coward.

**Leo** We're a pair of cowards, then?

**Bridget** You're not supposed to say that, Leo. Compliment me. Tell me I'm getting younger by the year. Remark on the way I've kept my figure. Jesus, that's the last time I'm going into a dark depression with you. You would put years on a body. How does Margaret stick you?

**Leo** Thanks for your sympathy.

**Bridget** What good does sympathy do for you?

**Leo** It lightens the load.

**Bridget** It does in your hole. I've never felt an ounce of sympathy in my life. That's how I've kept my looks. If I wish anyone well, I wish them a hard heart. Don't tell me you're soft carmels. The poor eejits drinking in your pubs – you'd take their last shilling. That's how you built your mansion in Dublin. This place didn't come cheap when you finished with it. Don't look at me for sympathy. You'll find none.

**Leo** You would have made a wonderful reverend mother.

**Bridget** Nuns are brides of Christ. I am a bride of Satan.

**Leo** You never invited us.

**Bridget** There was no wedding breakfast as such. What would you serve to the Devil? Hot and cold shite? We've been together some years now. We've been happy in our own way. I don't deny he can be a difficult man, but there are many times he's a little dote. I can make him laugh. Jokes, songs, unspeakable things with a burning coal. We're a normal Irish couple, the Prince of Darkness and his darling wife. Darby and Joan, me and Lucifer.

We've never believed in divorce either. In that respect we're devout Catholics.

**Leo** How come we never see you together?

**Bridget** He's painfully shy – he dislikes publicity. People always bring up –

*She does a downward movement with her fingers.*

You know, the whole heaven thing.

**Leo** The banishment – the fall –

**Bridget** It happened years ago. Why are they obsessed by it? We're not keen to talk about it. The other angels – the ones who fell with him – they can shoot their mouths off. My fella prefers to keep a dignified silence.

**Leo** Does he know me, Satan?

**Bridget** He knows everybody.

**Leo** Does he know my son?

*Silence.*

Does he hear my son cry? Is my boy weeping in hell? Does the Devil take any pity on him? Will Satan do what God won't do for me? Will he give me back my child?

*Silence.*

Will you ask him to do that?

**Bridget** I have, he can't help. Gene was dead. He, Satan, did not believe in resurrections. That was the other boyo's business. Pray to him for miracles of that order. But I explained it was unlikely you believed. He was glad. You would be wasting your time. For nobody's listening.

**Leo** He's as bleak as that?

**Bridget** Bleaker. Especially at the Christmas. Takes very badly to the drink. Raging that nobody remembers when it's his birthday.

**Leo** When was he born?

**Bridget** Every day of the year. There at all our shoulders, the hour, the minute you're born, plotting badness, taking child from parent, stealing, leading them astray, filling them with poison, putting the knife in their hand, cutting their beautiful flesh, leaving them alone to breathe their last, to be found dead by an old woman.

**Leo** I'm glad it was you.

**Bridget** While I live, I won't forget him.

**Leo** Thank you.

**Bridget** You're still a way to go.

**Leo** I'm near the end.

**Bridget** It will never end. It will only seem like it. Just when you think it's stopped, the pain, it starts again.

**Leo** How do you know this?

**Bridget** I don't. I'm guessing. Will you sell the house?

**Leo** I don't know yet.

**Bridget** If you decide to sell, you could give it away. Give it to me.

**Leo** You have a house.

**Bridget** A wee hovel. I could do with another. A bit more spacious.

**Leo** For you and Satan?

**Bridget** You didn't fall for that old shite, did you?

**Leo** Bridget, I always fall for what you tell me.

**Bridget** God, aren't you the right innocent. Just as well you're rich, just as well you're lucky.

**Leo** Sometimes luck runs out.

**Bridget** Run after it. Catch up with it. Who knows what you'll find.

**Leo** My son?

**Bridget** The boy is dead. How often do you have to be told? He won't be coming back. Will you stop torturing him? Stop torturing yourself. You might never be rid of him, but will you let him go from you? Stop haunting him. Set him free.

**Leo** I can't do that.

**Bridget** Then you'll have no comfort.

**Leo** Do I want it?

**Bridget** No, I see you don't. What do you want?

**Leo** My son.

*Silence.*

My son. I've lost my son. My child is dead.

*He begins to weep.*

Myself, and my son.

*The weeping is now fierce.*

Forgive me.

*He stops weeping.*

The light's gone out.

**Bridget** Put it back on again.

**Leo** When?

**Bridget** Now.

**Leo** I'll try.

**Bridget** You better.

**Leo** I will.

**Bridget** Fuck it, I hate crying. Especially my own. My face looks like a rubber sheet in an orphanage. Now, have you any food left over you'd like to give me?

**Leo** That's Margaret's department. You'll have to ask her.

*Louise and Simon enter the causeway.*
*They enter the house.*

**Bridget** Is she speaking to me?

*Margaret enters and stays in the causeway.*

**Leo** Ask them – they're back.

**Bridget** Hello, everybody – did you enjoy your stroll?

**Louise** Don't talk to me, you.

**Bridget** What did I do?

**Simon** What did you not do?

**Bridget** I was only trying to do my best –

**Simon** Leaving a bomb in the house.

**Bridget** Bombs – what are you saying – I have nothing to do with bombs –

**Louise** You're a bad bitch, lady.

**Simon** You knew the havoc you'd cause.

**Bridget** If I caused bother, I'm sorry – forgive me. Your father has. He was going to sell the house. I've begged him not to. Can you imagine losing this beautiful place? He says now he's not going to. It was me forced him. You owe me for that. We're quits.

**Simon** You're a fucking witch, Bridget.

**Bridget** No, I'm not – I'm more of a confused fairy. I really don't know if I'm coming or going.

**Louise** We're going – I've had enough of you. The car's packed. I want to be on the road early. Simon's coming with me.

**Simon** How long till you and Ma –

**Leo** Set off? Soon.

**Louise** You driving?

**Leo** I think so.

**Louise** Right. Bye, Dad.

*She kisses him.*
*She kisses Bridget.*

Goodbye, witch.

*She exits to the causeway.*

**Simon** See you, Dad. Love you.

*He kisses Leo.*
*Louise kisses Margaret in the garden.*

**Louise** She's not too contrite.

**Margaret** Surprise, surprise.

*Simon kisses Bridget.*

**Simon** Bad woman.

*He exits.*

**Bridget** Pair of fuckers.

**Louise** Ring us when you get home.

**Margaret** I will.

*Louise exits.*
*Margaret and Simon embrace.*
*Simon exits.*

**Bridget** What were they doing, kissing me? I should have slapped them round the gob. Children – Jesus, people who lived long ago in the caves had the right idea. Leave them at the side of the mountain to cry at night and let the luckiest survive. The rest would be eaten by wild beasts. Personally I feel sorry for the wolves that fed on them. They had slim pickings. Is that one outside not going to venture in?

*She raises her voice and calls out to Margaret.*

Are you not coming in here, or have I got plague?

*Margaret enters the house.*

**Margaret** We're packed and ready to go. There's food in the fridge.

**Bridget** Do you think I'd eat your leavings?

**Margaret** Yes, you would. And you kindly offered us yours.

**Bridget** My leavings?

**Margaret** The letter. He left it for you to find. For safe keeping. You did a fine job. He was right to trust you with it. He knew you'd be first to find him. He did die in your arms. That must have been his gift to you. I'm proud that in his last act he did pity you. He knew you'd never have a child alive in your arms. If you couldn't give life, he'd give you his death. That's how sorry he felt for you. Opposite to myself. Me, I feel no sorrow – no pity – no anger at you. What are you? A mad old bitch festering by her fire. That's all you are. All you have is your insanity. Do you know, I envy you. Living in this wilderness, you have your life ordered. You have everything sewn up. Yes, I'm jealous of you. So jealous, you should leave my house, leave my family, leave my sight. Never contact us again. Goodbye.

**Bridget** I have only two things to say to you in reply. First, after all your years in Dublin, isn't it great the way you never lost the Donegal lilt? What age must you be now? Well over fifty if you're a day. That's why I've something else to say. Would you not think your hair might look a lot better done up in a bun? I hope you don't mind me commenting on your style, but isn't that what a friend does?

*Silence.*

Am I not a friend?

**Margaret** You are not.

**Bridget** I will not stay where I am not wanted.

**Margaret** Then leave.

**Bridget** I am your relation, Leo. Are you going to let her say things like that to me?

**Leo** Leave us for a while, Bridget. Don't go too far.

*Bridget exits from the house, the buggy before her. She sits on a seat.*

**Margaret** Are you ready to drive back?

**Leo** I know she's a bad bitch, but you were very hard –

**Margaret** Not as hard as she deserved.

**Leo** Do you judge us all –

**Margaret** As I judge myself? I try to. What about you? How do you judge yourself?

**Leo** I find myself wanting.

**Margaret** And Gene – what about him?

**Leo** I looked into his coffin the morning of his funeral. I said something to him that nobody heard. I've not told you nor Simon nor Louise.

**Margaret** What did you tell him?

**Leo** I told him if I were given one wish, I would go back in time to before he was born and I would not change him, Gene, I would still choose him. I would not change my child, no matter what.

**Margaret** You loved him that much?

**Leo** I did.

**Margaret** So did I.

*They embrace.*
*They kiss.*
*They help each other to keep standing.*

What is going to become of us?

**Leo** I don't know.

**Margaret** We have to keep going.

**Leo** We do.

**Margaret** Are you all right?

**Leo** Is the car packed?

**Margaret** Everything.

**Leo** Bridget?

**Margaret** What about her?

**Leo** Say something as you leave.

**Margaret** What?

**Leo** Anything.

*She leaves the house and enters the causeway.*
*Bridget is still sitting there.*
*Leo fetches food from the fridge.*
*Margaret goes to Bridget.*
*She runs her fingers through Bridget's hair.*

**Margaret** Mind the house for us, you wicked wagon.

**Bridget** I will – I'm sorry.

**Margaret** You should be. Don't let the place burn to the ground. If it does, see that you're in it.

**Bridget** I will. See you soon.

**Margaret** Soon.

*Margaret exits.*
*Leo enters and puts the bag of food in the buggy.*

**Bridget** She's not as angry with me, is she?

**Leo** She's fairly angry, lady.

**Bridget** She's tired. She's not slept right. You do the driving. She'll be less crabbit when she gets to Dublin. It has something to do with the street lights. I'm told they're very soothing on the nerves. Not that I'd know. I've never been asked there to see them.

*She looks at the bag of food and lifts it.*

Is that all you've left me? Jesus, you've opened your arse.

**Leo** That is your gettings. Take it or leave it. I've slipped a few bob in the bag as well.

**Bridget** Thanks – I'm sure that will keep me in fur coats.

**Leo** You're an ungrateful fucker, aren't you?

**Bridget** If you want gratitude, look elsewhere. Have you not learned that much?

**Leo** The hard way.

**Bridget** Then at least he's done you that bit of good. Run on to swanky Dublin. I'll stay here. I'll mind him.

**Leo** He's not here – he's dead.

**Bridget** I think that point has been made with sufficient frequency to render it redundant. There is no necessity to repeat it. I am not deaf. Run on. Put a smile on the sour face of your wife. How much money did you leave me?

**Leo** What you're worth.

**Bridget** Is that all? God, you're tight. Will I see you soon? All of yous? Will you come down to visit soon?

**Leo** Soon.

**Bridget** I miss you. It's lonely.

**Leo** All lonely.

**Bridget** Safe journey.

**Leo** Aye, safe. I'll lock up. I have the keys. Safe journey.

*Leo exits.*
*Bridget stands up to look about her, singing.*

**Bridget**
There came a gypsy riding, riding, riding,
There came a gypsy riding –

*She starts to push the buggy.*

Marry all your children, children, children,
Marry all your children –

*There is a fierce cry of seabirds.*
*The swell of the sea.*
*She stands still and speaks.*

Don't weep. No need to. Listen to the rain and the wind. They do the crying. They are your epitaph.

*She sings as she stands.*

Here's your sixpence, here's your ring,
Goodbye, children, goodbye.
Goodbye, children, goodbye.